The Puffin Book of Improbable Records

Compiled by
Quentin Blake and
John Yeoman

and illustrated
by
Quentin Blake

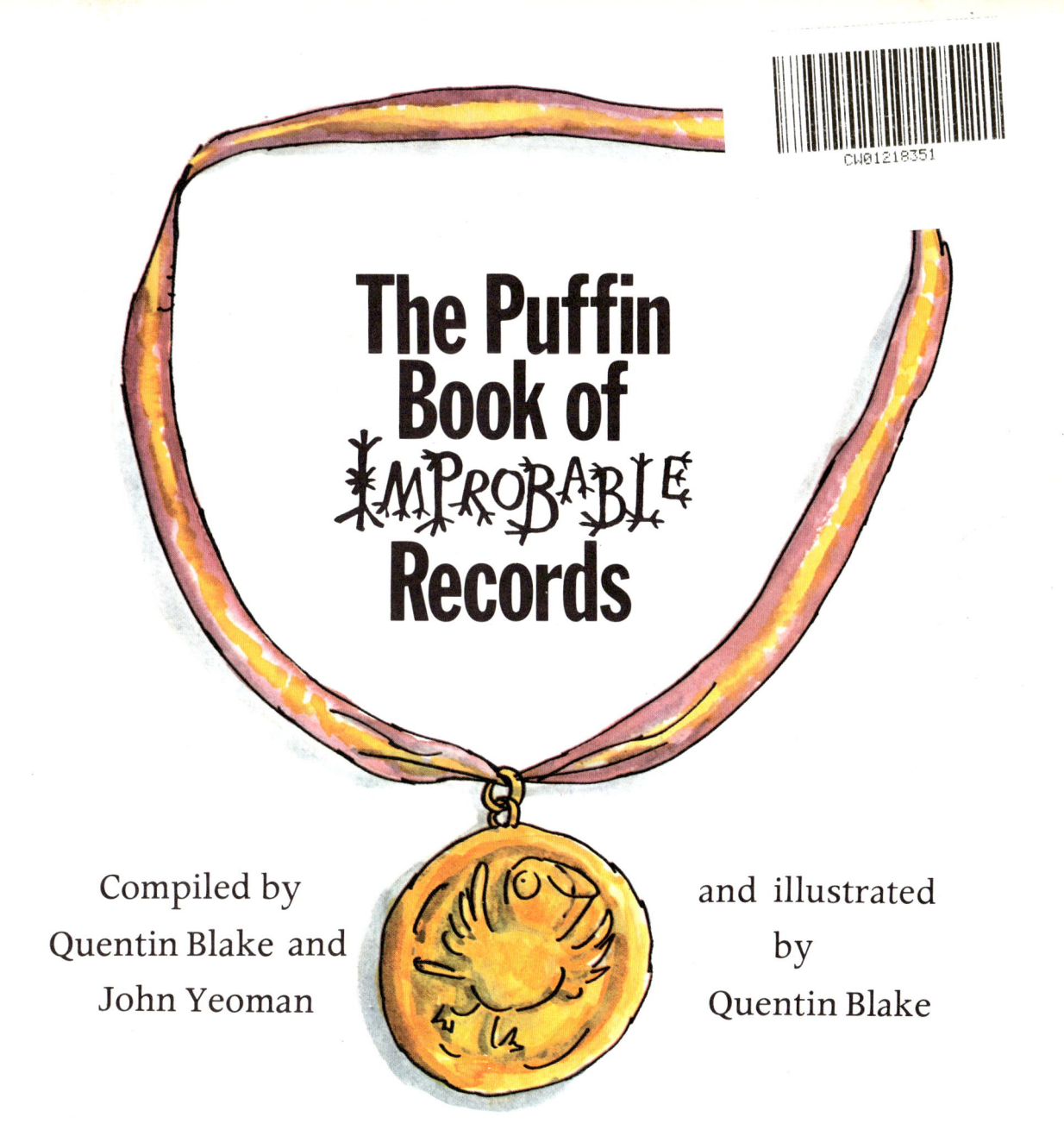

Puffin Books

The compilers at work on another record

AMAZING FACTS ABOUT THIS BOOK

Did you know:

- that *The Puffin Book of Improbable Records* is the only book to be issued to all Her Majesty's Forces as part of their survival kit on account of the high nutritional value of its paper and printing ink?
- that the compilers between them covered 18,291 miles by funicular railway, sedan chair, and bathyscope to collect their astounding information?
- that while at work on this book the compilers ate 4,978 bacon sandwiches and drank 9,983 mugs of cocoa?
- that while doing the pictures for this book Quentin Blake 48 times dipped his brush into the mug of cocoa instead of into the paint water?

— that 17 times he drank the paint water instead of the mug of cocoa?

— that if everyone gave a copy of *The Puffin Book of Improbable Records* to all their friends, the world would be a happier place, especially for Quentin Blake and John Yeoman?

— that if you piled all the existing copies of *The Puffin Book of Improbable Records* in the middle of Oxford Street, the police would arrest you for causing an obstruction?

Important Note:

The compilers of this book acknowledge that, though they have taken great pains to verify all the following records, some slight errors of fact may have crept in unavoidably.

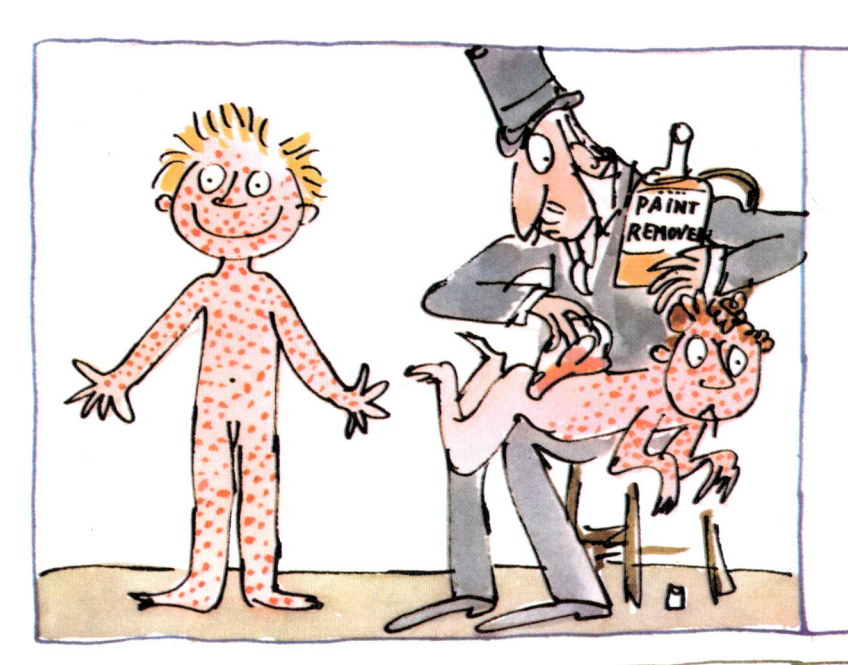

Jimmy Fluff, aged 11, was proclaimed British record holder at the Crystal Palace chicken-pox spots competition of 1903, after the judge had declared the other principal contestant guilty of cheating.

Some of the astounding 485 umbrellas that Miss Angela Fraill of Woking has left behind on public transport since she began travelling alone in 1937.

The record for standing up to the waist in water in the Manchester Ship Canal is held by Titus Wellington, who stood there for 835 hours during one particularly mild April.

The world's most hopeless daily help was Eliza Widdershins of East Penge. In one day alone, in May 1923, she broke a complete Crown Derby tea-service while washing up, reduced the weekly wash to shreds, and absent-mindedly threw the baby into the dustbin.

The most hairy spider in the world was 'Wuffles', a giant tarantula belonging to Mrs Bernstein of São Paulo. He received many prizes including the coveted Osgood Award at the International Congress of Hairiness in 1893.

Mr Thrimble's Potato

The real Queen Victoria

A potato bearing a striking resemblance to Queen Victoria was grown by Mr Norbert Thrimble of Strood. An unconfirmed report has it that the potato, suitably dressed, stood in for Her Majesty on a number of rather boring royal functions.

The longest strip of postage stamps ever to come out of one machine was bought by Mr Adam Senilitude of Old Sarum, who used his meagre life-savings, all in coins, for that purpose.

The largest collection of cats ever to be housed in one bedsittingroom was owned by Miss Felicity Parminter-Lloyd, who, though desperately shortsighted, never lost an opportunity to rescue a stray from the streets. At one time she owned 167.

The only centipede with a hundred and one legs was recorded in Sidcup by Dr Arnold Mibsby in 1952.

The most difficult code in the world was invented by J. X. Griswold in 1944. He refused to reveal its secret to a single person and has now forgotten it himself.

Fiona MacSomething of Ballachulish became the youngest Bagpipe Champion of the Highlands in 1934 at only 9 years of age. She was persuaded to pursue her studies at the Royal Academy of Music in London when it was discovered that her playing was killing the sheep in Ballachulish.

At the age of 47, Mr Endymion Crust of Widnes holds the record for getting into cinemas half-price.

A sausage at St Cynthia's School in West Drayton has been served for school dinner 8,947 times and returned uneaten on each occasion.

The most rapid take-off for a hot-air balloon was achieved by Noldley Stokes on Primrose Hill in 1889, when his assistant released the final mooring cable before Mr Stokes had finished saying good-bye to his parents.

Amateur wax-modeller Origen Pest of Utah made 83 life-size effigies of himself out of candle ends.

The real Origen Pest

The largest Irish family (total weight 890·4 kilos) to cross Oxford Street on a tightrope was the O'Shaunnessy family from Tipperary.

In 1937 the British Post Office Parcel Crunching Competition was won by Postman George O. Filbert who set an all-time record. He scored 986 points, with a Silver Medal in the 'Fragile – Handle with Care' section.

The oldest international cross-country unicyclist was Sir Geoffrey Treacle of Treacle Hall in Derbyshire. After fifty years of unicycling he won the gruelling Alpine open competition on his 80th birthday in 1893, including the world speed record for the ascent of Mont Blanc.

One of the finalists in the ballroom-dancing championship of 1962, Mrs Berenice Stoll of Deptford, sewed a grand total of 16,449 sequins on to her dress. Unfortunately, her husband Tancred was unable to lift such a weight from the floor.

The most brilliant banana-balancer of all time was Pierre Strapontin, captain of the French banana-balancing team and unbeaten world-champion for twenty years until his retirement in 1907.

The banana-balancing endurance record is held by Ron Fudge of Idaho, who balanced a banana on his nose for twenty-seven days in 1928.

The longest distance travelled by a human cannonball is 793 metres, a record established by the Great Volario who left the grounds of Bodling Brothers Circus at Blye and ended up on the tower of St Mary's-in-the-Tansy.

The world's soppiest fairy-story is *Cuddly-Bunnikins and Little Fairy Twinklewand* by Emily Tichweed. On the left: Miss Tichweed and her pet rabbit, Cecil.

The largest number of hedgehogs to do a perfect forward roll in succession was 179, at Scrimshaw's Gymnasium in Balham in 1903.

The longest football supporters' scarf ever made (just over 7·2 km long) was knitted by Victorine Plum of Solihull. It began as a sock but she couldn't master the art of turning the heel.

The world record for highly polished floors is held by Eileen O'Flaherty, an office cleaner for a firm of reputable solicitors in Sydney, Australia. At her peak, the entire office staff had been known to fall over on her gleaming floors.

The elephant with the shortest memory was Alfred, of Bunfield's Travelling Zoo. He could never remember where he had put anything.

The only duck to wear plimsolls is Hodge, of Compton Martin in Somerset. He is afraid of getting his feet wet.

The friendliest woodlouse in the world is called Sidney. He has 985 friends.

The worst mousetrap in the world was made by the German inventor Gerhard von Rauchenverboten in 1453. It weighed 365 kilos and took two men three-quarters of an hour to wind up. It contained 1·36 kilos of best Bavarian smoked cheese, but it was so slow that it never caught any mice.

The world's strangest pet belongs to Rodney Smithers of Eltham, who owns the Fanged Beast from Planet X.

The highest jump by a flea with a wooden leg was recorded at the last professional appearance of the Amazing Waldo in Mainz in 1923. It is still known among circus folk as 'Waldo's Farewell'.

The heaviest wedding-cake – which weighed just over one-third of a tonne – was made for Mr and Mrs Arnold Piping of Oswestry by Mr Eddy Flin, ex-sergeant major of the Royal Army Catering Corps.

The man with the most letters after his name is Professor Sir Cosmo Bacillus MA, PhD, LLB, KGB, MP, FRS, OM, VC, MC, PS, RSVP, NB, PTO, OAP, BBC, WD, QED, PVC, LMS, MOT, OHMS, ARP, BO, KO, DDT, PAYE, VAT, MCC, TNT, DIY, JP, MO, DV, RIP, OK, HP, GLC, TCP, SOS, SWALK, (Continued on page 47).

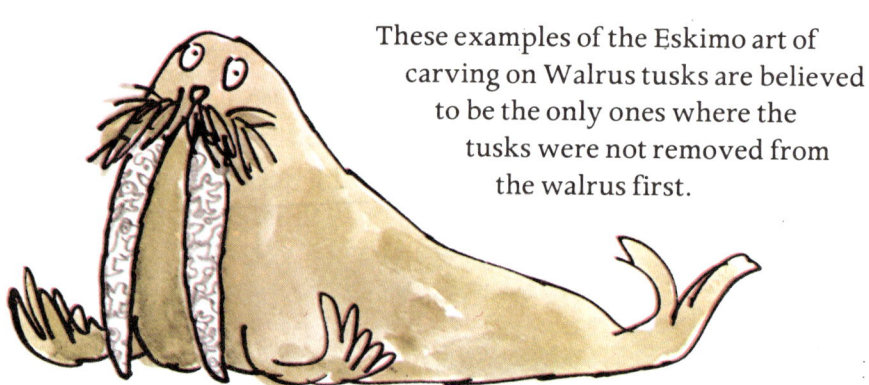

The largest quantity of carrot wine ever to be made in a London basement flat was produced by the Armitage family of Kensal Green. They turned out 6,529 bottles, of which they sold four.

These examples of the Eskimo art of carving on Walrus tusks are believed to be the only ones where the tusks were not removed from the walrus first.

The all-time world champions of non-stop mouse-dancing were Charles and Nina (seen here with their trainer Mr Vance LeRoy). In the Transatlantic Mouse-dancing Marathon of 1928 in Palm Springs, Charles and Nina danced a tango for 983 hours.

The boy with the most disgusting table manners was Terry Wormold of Shropshire. In parts of Shropshire mothers still tell their children to 'stop Wormolding'.

Mr Ethelbert Soames of Erith holds the record for wearing a fancy dress costume. He refused to take it off after a party at Christmas 1947, since when he has lived entirely on lettuce.

Angelica and Lance Millichope hold the record for being the world's most unidentical twins.

A snake called Mervyn, belonging to a scout troop in Northampton, is the only one ever to have been trained to demonstrate knots.

Belisarius (born Dec. 1885 – exploded Jan. 1900), star performer of Moxom and Footling's Toad Circus, could hold his breath for 8 hours 43 minutes, in a self-induced trance.

The world's most obstinate donkey is Henrietta, of Margate Sands, who accepted her first customer in 1919 and hasn't budged since.

The only tone-deaf canary belongs to Mrs Nora Napkyn-Smith of Eastbourne. Despite expensive professional training it can only manage a hoarse squeak.

The most boring man in the world was Frederick Drone who, one evening at the Sandwich Club in 1903, sent 85 long-standing members into deep torpor while recounting his experiences of the Boer War. He is said not to have noticed.

⬅ The dirtiest player in professional football is reputed to be Eddie Bovver, who has represented his club in 87 matches but has spent only $14\frac{1}{2}$ minutes actually on the field.

A secret message written in the most invisible ink in the world, invented by Professor O. J. Flange in 1911.

The noisiest veteran car still on the road is a 1914 Musgrove Whirlwind belonging to Mr Alistair Whimbrel of Bath. At its full speed of 27 km ph it makes 176 distinct noises, including skreek, grunge, kdoink, blonk-blonk-blonk, flippety-flappety, ptwang and urrgggh.

Gipsy Rose Studholme, mother of four and part-time fortune-teller in Newcastle-under-Lyme, successfully predicted 139 cases of twisted ankle in succession.

The greatest number of artificial flowers ever assembled on one hat belonged to a Mrs Emily Woodbine of Chiswick, who wore the hat for 32 consecutive summers until, in July 1929, it succumbed to an appalling attack of greenfly and had to be destroyed.

The largest unfinished statue in the world was a symbolic figure of 'Progress' commissioned by Darlington Corporation from R. Figgis-Jones in 1899. Unfortunately funds ran out in 1901 when only the big toe of the left foot had been completed.

The first inflatable swimming aid was the Bickerstaff Brothers' Buoyancy Bathing Suit for Beginners (1865). Its usefulness was often questioned.

At the age of only $5\frac{1}{2}$ months Garfield Hebble had already bitten the fingers of 94 old ladies who had tried to tickle him under the chin as he lay in his pram outside Tesco's in Chester-le-Street.

The hamster with the most elastic cheek pouches was owned by Lucy Bonavia of Orpington, Kent. Lucy's hamster once excelled himself by consuming a whole Christmas stocking complete with presents.

The most awful smell in the world was at the corner of Mouse Lane and Mould Street in South London in February 1955. Scenes of panic followed until the smell gradually faded some days later.

The longest unpublished novel is currently being written by Eileen Penumbra who began the work – as a short story – in 1918 at the age of 15.

The parrot with the largest vocabulary is Sebastian of Wembley who knows the dictionary by heart.

sedentary [sedenteRi] *adj* habitually sitting still for long periods; requiring little bodily exertion; requiring or caused by sitting; (*zool*) not migratory.
sedge [sej] *n* coarse grass-like plant, *usu* growing beside water.
sedilia [sedili-a] *n* (*pl*) (*eccles*) three recessed seats within the altar rails.
sediment [sediment] *n* matter which sinks to the bottom of a liquid; dregs.
sedimentary [sedimenteRi] *adj* of or containing sediment; **s. rocks** rocks which have been deposited as beds, often by water.

Who's a lovely boy, then?

The hardest conker ever recorded belonged to Mr Edwin de Vaughn Sibthorpe, Captain of the Clerkenwell Solicitors' Conkers Team. It was a one-million-nine-thousand-two-hundred-and-seventy-sixer.

Lorenzo Romano

Signor Lorenzo Romano was the only man ever to have trained his moustache into the shape of his own signature. He received a special award at the Grand International Congress of Hairiness in Trieste in 1907.

The worst child ballet dancers in the world were Miss Treldiana Pelkey and the Hon. Miss Dorothea ffortescue-Wood. At one charity concert they tripped over 47 times, and finally fell off the stage altogether, injuring several members of the audience.

The book with the most ponies is *Sarah and her 4,983,297 ponies* by Irene Fetlock.

Lemuel Potter of New York owned a Caspian perch which made 42 partially successful attempts to escape from its aquarium. Science has been unable to provide an explanation of this bizarre phenomenon.

Mr Alfred Bight remained suspended 7·62 cm above the pavement in Kensington High Street for 8 hours 17 minutes in 1963, while holding the strings of 43 hydrogen-filled balloons which he was trying to sell.

⬆ The most musical door chimes were devised by Ned Cadenza of Birmingham, for his rather deaf grandmother, Mrs Alda Cadenza.

👉 Miss Wanda Hollyberry of Dorking Gap holds the record for having written the greatest number of letters asking if we couldn't possibly include her somewhere in *The Puffin Book of Improbable Records*.